Walter Foster
Jr.

learn to draw
Sea Creatures

Step-by-step instructions for more than 25 ocean animals

ILLUSTRATED BY ROBBIN CUDDY

Brimming with creative inspiration, how-to projects, and useful information to enrich your everyday life, Quarto Knows is a favorite destination for those pursuing their interests and passions. Visit our site and dig deeper with our books into your area of interest: Quarto Creates, Quarto Cooks, Quarto Homes, Quarto Lives, Quarto Drives, Quarto Explores, Quarto Gifts, or Quarto Kids.

© 2014 Quarto Publishing Group USA Inc.
Photographs © Shutterstock.

First published in 2014 by Walter Foster Jr., an imprint of The Quarto Group.
26391 Crown Valley Parkway, Suite 220, Mission Viejo, CA 92691, USA.
T (949) 380-7510 **F** (949) 380-7575 **www.QuartoKnows.com**

Walter Foster Jr. titles are also available at discount for retail, wholesale, promotional, and bulk purchase. For details, contact the Special Sales Manager by email at specialsales@quarto.com or by mail at The Quarto Group, Attn: Special Sales Manager, 100 Cummings Center, Suite 265D, Beverly, MA 01915, USA.

ISBN: 978-1-60058-445-9

Printed in China
20 19 18 17 16 15 14 13

Table of Contents

Tools & Materials

There's more than one way to bring sea creatures to life on paper—
you can use crayons, markers, colored pencils, or even paints.
Just be sure you have plenty of good "ocean colors"—
blue, purple, gray, brown, black, orange, and white.

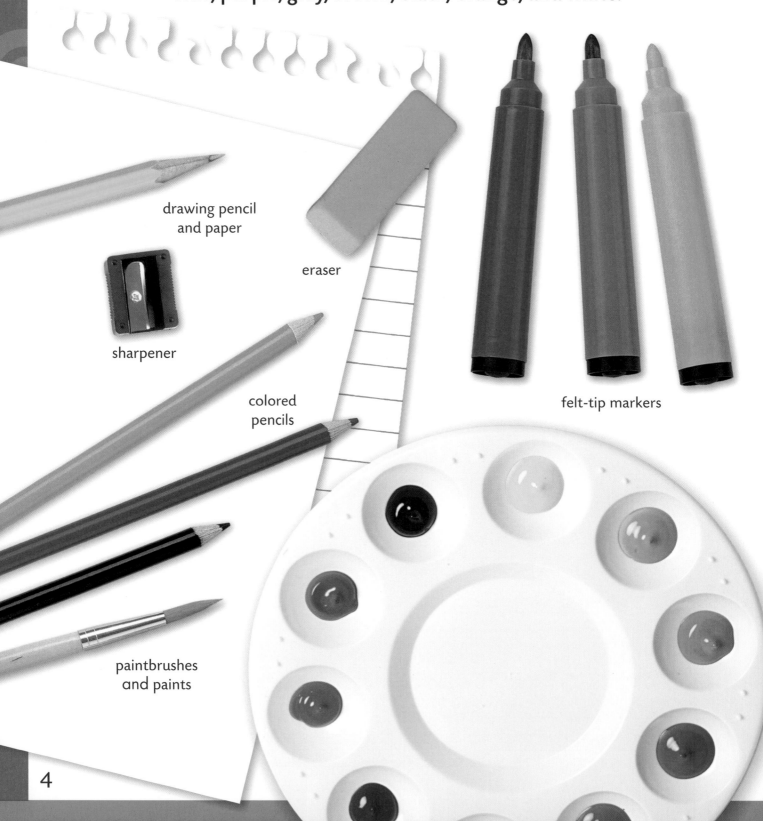

drawing pencil
and paper

eraser

sharpener

felt-tip markers

colored
pencils

paintbrushes
and paints

How to Use This Book

The drawings in this book are made up of basic shapes, such as circles, triangles, and rectangles. Practice drawing the shapes below.

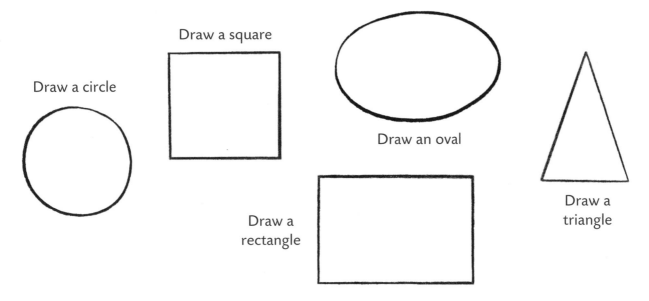

Draw a circle

Draw a square

Draw an oval

Draw a rectangle

Draw a triangle

Notice how these drawings begin with basic shapes.

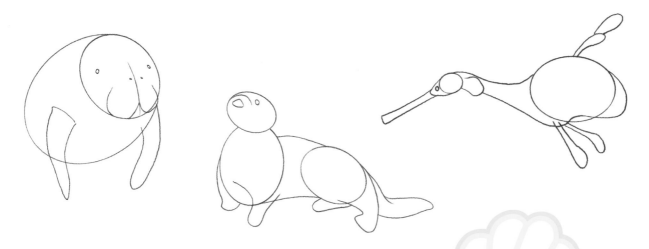

In this book, you'll learn about the size, location, diet, and appearance of each featured sea creature. Look for mini quizzes along the way to learn new and interesting facts!

Look for this symbol, and check your answers on page 64!

Classifications & Species

Sea Mammals

Marine mammals are divided into three orders: Carnivora, Cetacea, and Sirenia.

Order Carnivora

This order includes carnivorous sea mammals, such as sea lions, fur seals, true seals, walruses, and sea otters, as well as some land mammals like polar bears that depend on the ocean for the majority of their food.

Order Cetacea

This order includes all species that are completely aquatic and cannot survive on land, such as whales, dolphins, and porpoises.

Order Sirenia

This order includes species like manatees and dugongs that live in warm and tropical waters and feed on plant life.

Crustaceans

Crustaceans are invertebrate animals with several pairs of legs and an exoskeleton, such as crabs, lobsters, and shrimps.

Sea Reptiles

Marine reptiles, such as sea turtles and saltwater crocodiles, live in the ocean but return to land to lay their eggs.

Sharks

Sharks have streamlined bodies that help them move quickly in the water. While most sharks live in saltwater, there are a few species that live in both freshwater and saltwater.

Cephalopods

Squids, octopuses, and cuttlefish are classified as cephalopods. These animals are known for their large heads and long tentacles.

African Penguin

Size:
2 feet tall

Location:
Southwestern
Africa

Weight: 5
to 9 pounds

Diet: Small fish

Fun Fact!

African penguins live in large, noisy groups. Its call is similar to the bray of a donkey.

African penguins are small and round, with white bellies and legs. It has black feet, a black face, and a thin black band across the chest.

1

2

3

4

5

6

Did You Know?

The African penguin is an endangered species, with only 70,000 breeding pairs left in the wild. It is the only penguin that lives and breeds in Africa.

7

Blowfish

Size: Up to 3 feet in length

Diet: Algae, invertebrates, and some shellfish

Location: Warm oceans along the equator and subpolar regions

Fun Fact!

Blowfish are extremely poisonous, but some predators, such as sharks and sea snakes, are immune.

Blowfish have round bodies with sharp spines and large mouths that can suck in water and "puff" up their bodies as a defense against predators.

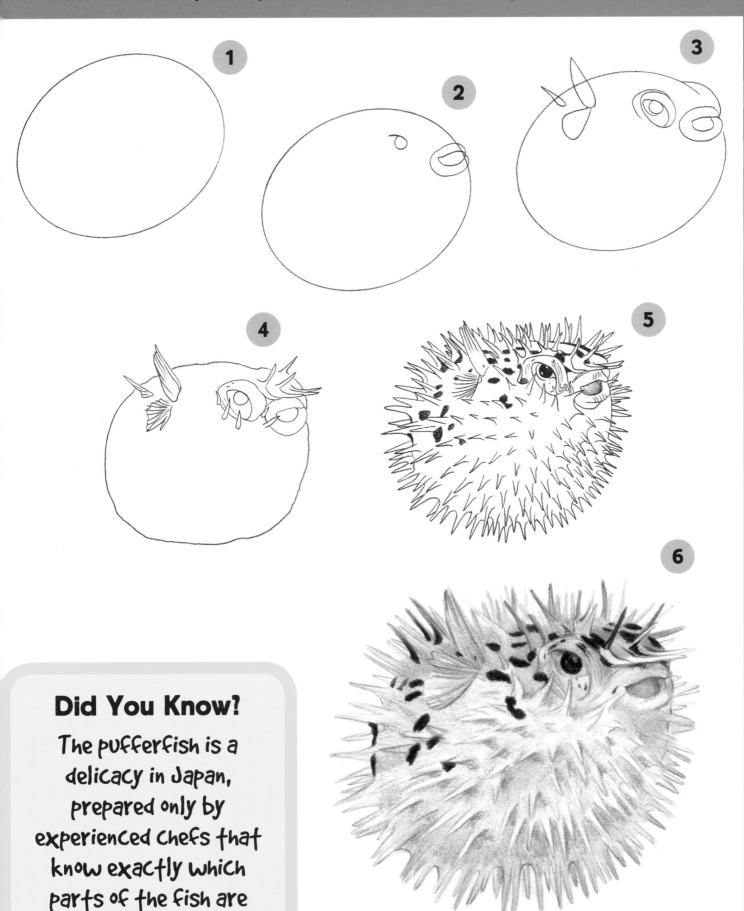

Did You Know?

The pufferfish is a delicacy in Japan, prepared only by experienced chefs that know exactly which parts of the fish are not poisonous.

Bottlenose Dolphin

Weight: 1,100 pounds

Size: 10 to 14 feet in length

Diet: Fish, shrimp, and squid

Did You Know?

Bottlenose dolphins are extremely intelligent and communicate with each other using a complex series of clicking noises and whistles.

Location: Along the coastlines of most equatorial and subpolar oceans

Bottlenose dolphins are long and sleek, with bottle-like snouts and sharp teeth.

1

2

3

4

5

6

7

Mini Quiz

What is the correct name for a family of dolphins?
A. Group
B. Pod
C. Herd
D. Swarm
(Answer on page 64)

Clownfish

Size: 3 to 5 inches in length

Did You Know?

The clownfish has a layer of mucus on its skin that protects it from an anemone's poison.

Location: Indian and Pacific Oceans

Diet: Parasites and food scraps from other fish

Clownfish are bright orange with three white stripes. They live within the poisonous barbs of sea anemones for protection.

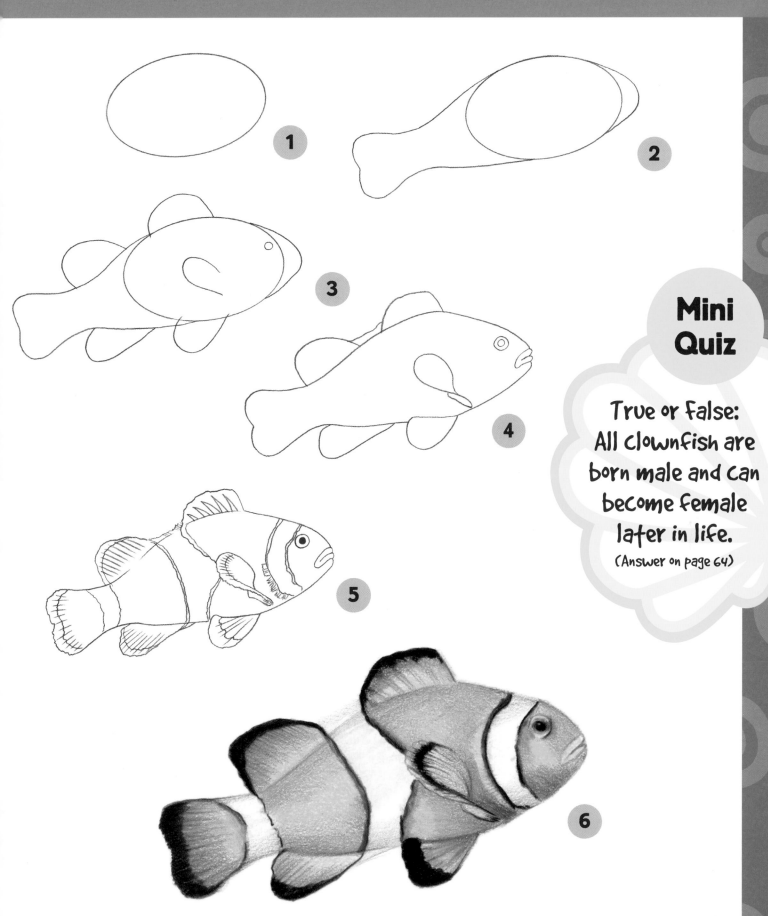

1

2

3

4

5

6

Mini Quiz

True or false: All clownfish are born male and can become female later in life.

(Answer on page 64)

Crab

Size: From a few millimeters up to 13 feet, crabs come in all shapes and sizes

Location: Crabs are found in freshwater and oceans all over the world, but small land crabs are usually found in tropical regions

Diet: Algae, invertebrates, and plants

Fun Fact!

Crabs have a hard exoskeleton. As the crab grows, it sheds its old exoskeleton and leaves the empty husk behind.

Land crabs come in a variety of sizes, but they all have a pair of small claws that they use to burrow into the sand on the beach or in the soil.

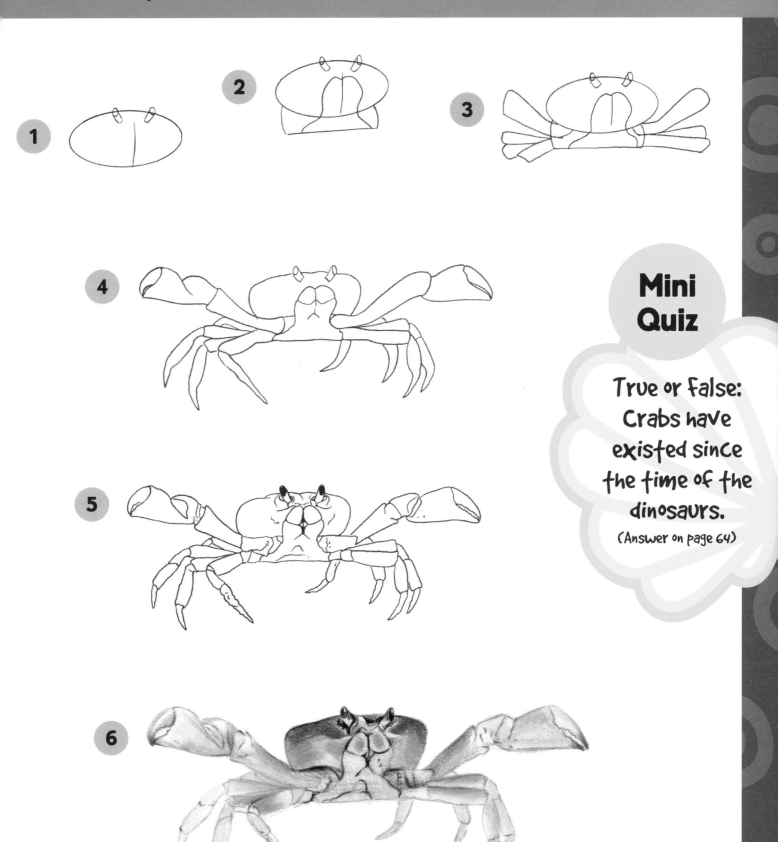

1

2

3

4

5

6

Mini Quiz

True or false: Crabs have existed since the time of the dinosaurs.

(Answer on page 64)

Great White Shark

Details

Size: 15 feet in length
Weight: Up to 5,000 pounds
Location: Coastal, temperate waters in the Pacific and Atlantic Oceans
Diet: Sea lions, seals, and small whales

Did You Know?

Great white sharks have many rows of razor-sharp teeth that are each up to 3 inches long. As teeth are lost or broken, new teeth from the underlying rows simply rotate into place.

The great white shark is the largest predatory fish in the ocean. It has more than 300 triangle-shaped teeth and a large dorsal fin on its back.

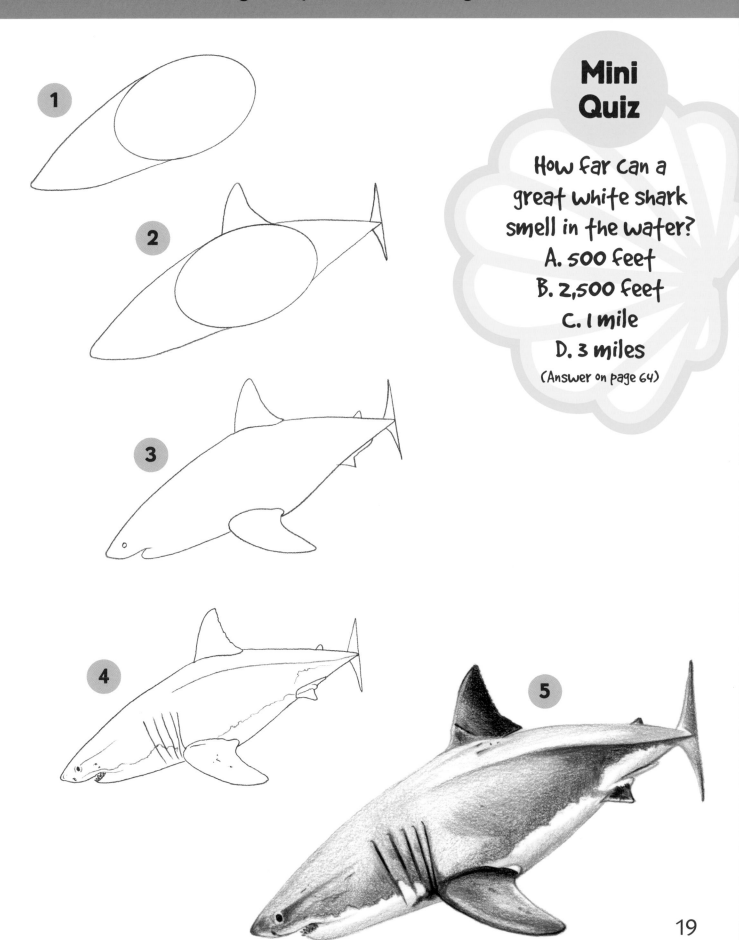

Mini Quiz

How far can a great white shark smell in the water?
A. 500 feet
B. 2,500 feet
C. 1 mile
D. 3 miles
(Answer on page 64)

Hammerhead Shark

Details

Size: 13 to 20 feet in length
Weight: Up to 1,000 pounds
Location: Warm, tropical ocean waters
Diet: Fish, squid, and stingrays

A hammerhead shark's elongated head contains sensitive organs that can find prey buried in the sandy ocean floor.

Fun Fact!

Hammerhead sharks are gray-brown to olive-green in color, with long, powerful bodies and flat, mallet-shaped heads.

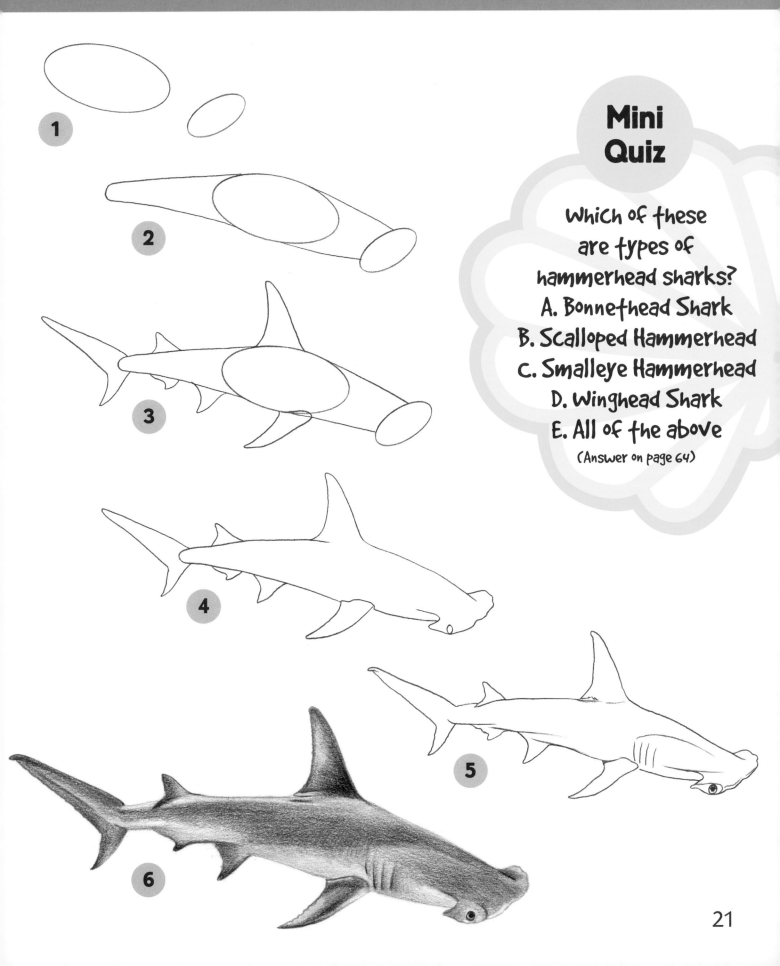

Mini Quiz

Which of these are types of hammerhead sharks?
A. Bonnethead Shark
B. Scalloped Hammerhead
C. Smalleye Hammerhead
D. Winghead Shark
E. All of the above
(Answer on page 64)

21

Jellyfish

Details

Size: 1 to 16 inches in length
Location: All oceans, usually found drifting along coastlines
Diet: Fish, shrimp, plants, and even other jellyfish!

Did You Know?

There are more than 200 species of jellyfish in the ocean. They have hundreds of tiny, stinging cells in their tentacles that they use to defend themselves and catch food.

Jellyfish are invertebrates, meaning they have no skeleton. They have soft, round bodies and long tentacles that float beneath them.

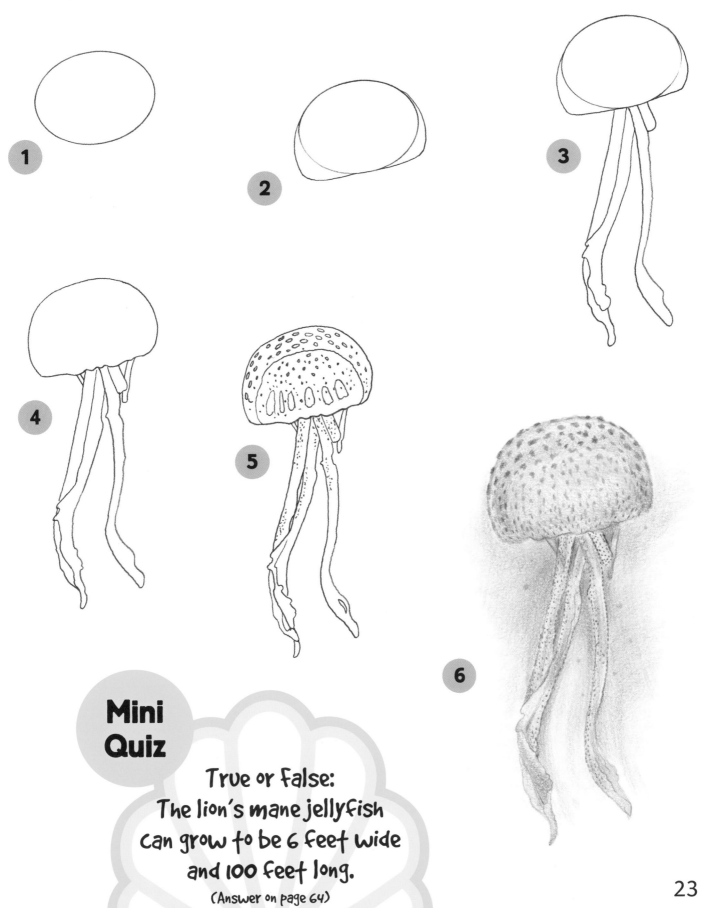

Mini Quiz

True or false:
The lion's mane jellyfish
can grow to be 6 feet wide
and 100 feet long.
(Answer on page 64)

Leafy Sea Dragon

Details

Size: Up to 14 inches in length
Location: Coastal waters of southern Australia
Diet: Plankton and very small shrimp and fish

Fun Fact!

Leafy sea dragons have tiny fins that help guide them among kelp and seaweed beds, but mostly they simply float along with the ocean currents.

Leafy sea dragons are related to sea horses and have leaf-shaped appendages that help camouflage them among the seaweed beds.

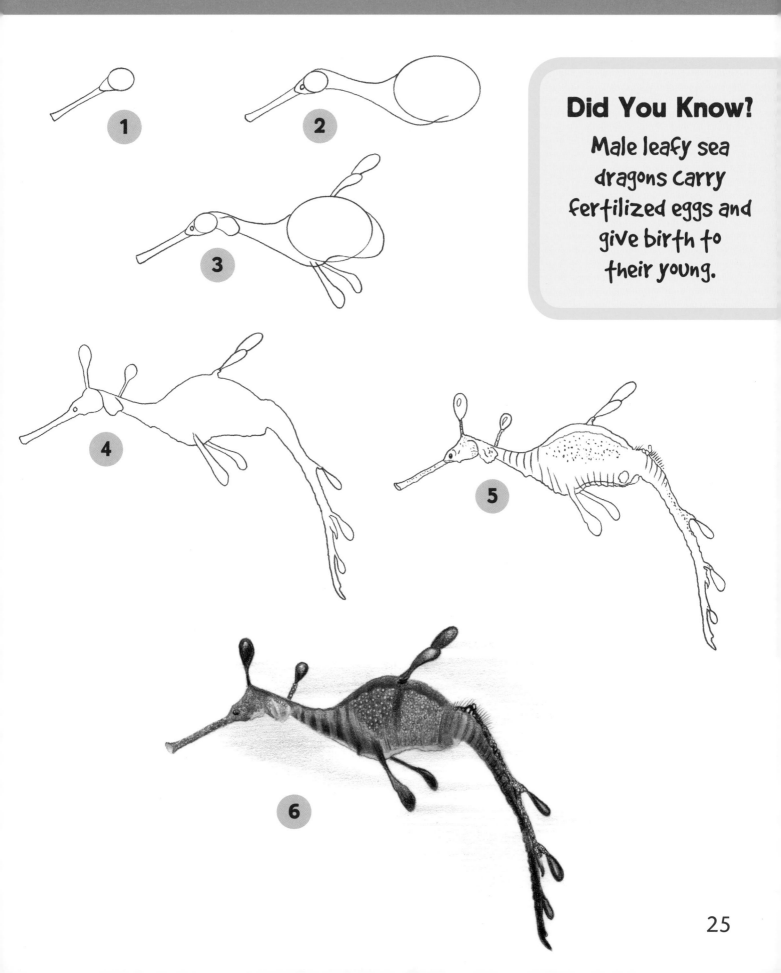

Did You Know?
Male leafy sea dragons carry fertilized eggs and give birth to their young.

1

2

3

4

5

6

Manatee

Details

Size: 8 to 13 feet in length
Weight: Up to 1,300 pounds
Location: Tropical and subtropical Atlantic coastlines, rivers, and lagoons
Diet: Water grasses, weeds, and algae

Did You Know?

Early explorers and sailors often mistook manatees for mermaids.

Also known as sea cows, manatees have two front flippers and a large, powerful tail that helps propel them forward in the water.

Mini Quiz

How fast can manatees swim?
A. 5 miles per hour
B. 10 miles per hour
C. 15 miles per hour
D. 30 miles per hour
(Answer on page 64)

Moray Eel

Location: Tropical and subtropical oceans

Size: Up to 13 feet in length

Weight: Up to 30 pounds

Diet: Fish and a variety of crabs, squid, and mollusks

Fun Fact!

Moray eels have two sets of teeth! One set is in the mouth for catching prey, and the other is in the throat and is used for digestion.

Moray eels have long, sleek bodies with thick, smooth skin. They hide in small caves among coral reefs and have large jaws with sharp teeth.

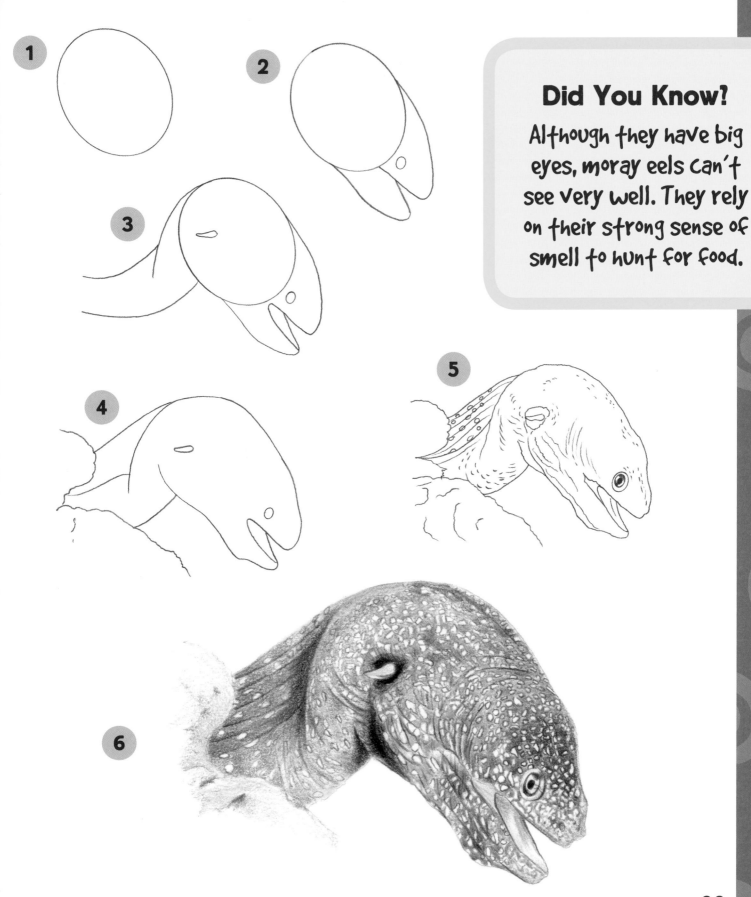

Did You Know?

Although they have big eyes, moray eels can't see very well. They rely on their strong sense of smell to hunt for food.

Octopus

Details

Size: 1 to 3 feet in length
Weight: Up to 20 pounds
Location: Tropical coastal ocean waters around the world
Diet: Crabs, crayfish, and mollusks

Did You Know?

An octopus can change its colors to match those around it, camouflaging itself among the rocks and colorful corals where it lives.

An octopus has a large, round head; eight long, curling legs; and a small, hard beak hidden underneath its body.

Fun Fact!

An octopus is an invertebrate, which allows it to easily hide within small caves and coral reefs.

Orca Whale

Size: 20 to 30 feet in length
Weight: Up to 6 tons
Location: Cold, coastal waters from polar regions to the equator
Diet: Seals, sea lions, fish, and sometimes even small whales

Did You Know?

Orcas are actually large dolphins—not whales at all!

Orcas, also known as "killer whales," have long dorsal fins and are mostly black with white underbellies and patches near the eyes.

Mini Quiz

Orcas communicate through a series of whistles and sounds called:
A. Echolocation
B. Doppler
C. Pulsar
D. Whale-speak
(Answer on page 64)

Pelican

Size: 5 feet in length, with a 10-foot wingspan

Diet: Fish

Location: Coastlines around the world

Fun Fact!

Pelicans fish in groups, helping each other round up fish in shallow waters along the coastline.

34

Did You Know?

Some pelicans can hold more than 3 gallons of water in their throat pouches!

Pelicans are large birds with long, slender beaks and large pouches in their throats used for scooping up and carrying fish to their young.

Queen Angelfish

Size: Up to 18 inches in length

Diet: Sponges, algae, and jellyfish

Location: Caribbean and western Atlantic Oceans

Fun Fact!

Angelfish often gather food by cleaning small parasites off of other larger fish.

Did You Know?

Queen angelfish have a blue ring on their heads that looks like a crown.

The angelfish has bright, beautiful colors that help it hide among the colorful reefs where it lives.

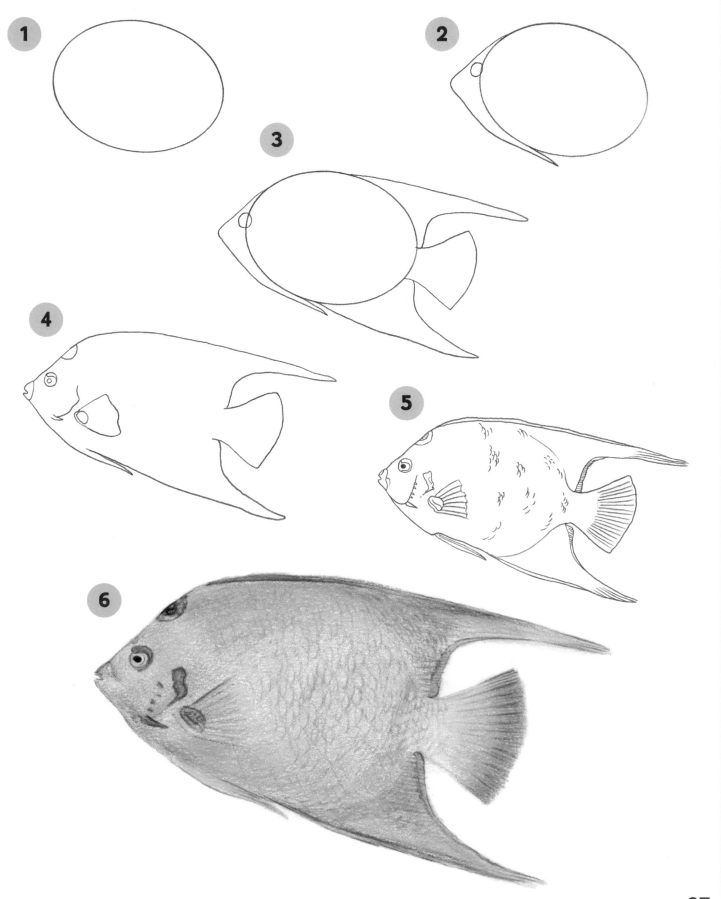

Royal Blue Tang

Size: 8 to 12 inches in length

Diet: Algae and small shrimp

Location: Atlantic and Pacific Oceans

Did You Know?

Young blue tangs are mostly yellow with blue spots near their eyes. As they grow, they become more and more blue.

Royal blue tangs are a deep blue with black markings and a bright yellow tail. They have flat bodies with pointed, beak-like mouths.

Mini Quiz

True or False:
Royal blue tangs are also called "surgeonfish" because they have sharp spines on either side of their tails.

(Answer on page 64)

Sea Horse

Details

Size: 2 to 35 centimeters in length
Location: Along the coastlines of most oceans
Diet: Plankton and small brine shrimp

Did You Know?

Sea horses use their long tails to grip seaweed and corals along the ocean floor.

Sea horses have horse-shaped heads and pointy snouts. They are poor swimmers, and they float along in the ocean currents, steered only by a tiny fin on their backs.

Fun Fact!

Just like horses, a group of sea horses is called a "herd."

Sea Lion

Details

Size: 6 to 7 feet in length
Weight: 230 to 800 pounds
Location: Subarctic oceans, but some prefer the warmer waters of the coastal Pacific Ocean
Diet: Fish, crabs, and squid

Fun Fact!

Sea lions are very social and intelligent. They travel in large groups and enjoy "talking" to each other in loud, noisy colonies on land.

Sea lions have two long flippers in front and two shorter ones in back. They are strong swimmers, but they can also hop about on land.

Did You Know!

Sea lions' whiskers are important for hunting! Each whisker has its own nerve ending to help the sea lion swim and hunt.

Sea Otter

Details

Size: 4 feet in length
Weight: 35 to 90 pounds
Location: Along the coasts of the northern Pacific Ocean
Diet: Shellfish, sea urchins, crabs, squid, and fish

Did You Know?

Sea otters live almost entirely in water, floating contentedly on their backs in coastal kelp beds. They constantly clean their bodies so that their fur stays waterproof against the cold.

Sea otters have thick, waterproof fur; wide, flipper-like webbed feet; and tiny, short ears and nostrils that close when swimming.

Fun Fact!

Sea otters break open mussels and clams using small rocks balanced on their chests.

Sea Snail

Size: From 1 millimeter to 3 feet in length

Location: Saltwater oceans around the world

Diet: Plants and algae

Fun Fact!

The world's largest sea snail is the Australian trumpet, which can grow up to 3 feet in length and weigh up to 40 pounds!

Sea snails grow their own spiral- or cone-shaped shells, which help protect them from predators.

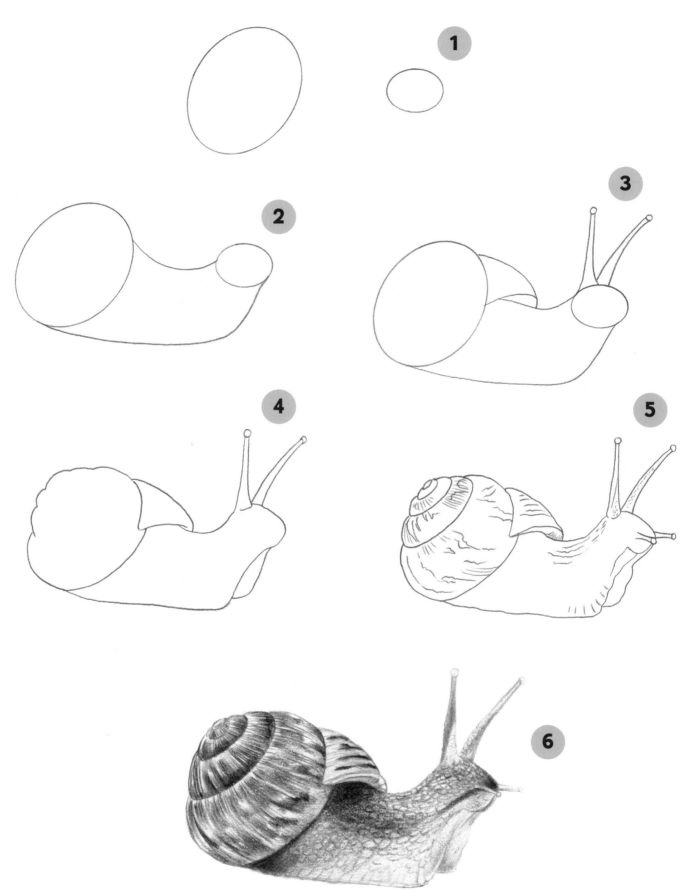

Sea Turtle

Details

Size: Up to 5 feet in length
Weight: Up to 700 pounds
Location: Tropical and subtropical coastal oceans
Diet: Sea grasses, algae, crabs, and jellyfish

Fun Fact!

Sea turtles can live as long as humans! They are known to live an average of 80 years or longer.

One of the oldest creatures in the world, green sea turtles have existed since before the dinosaurs.

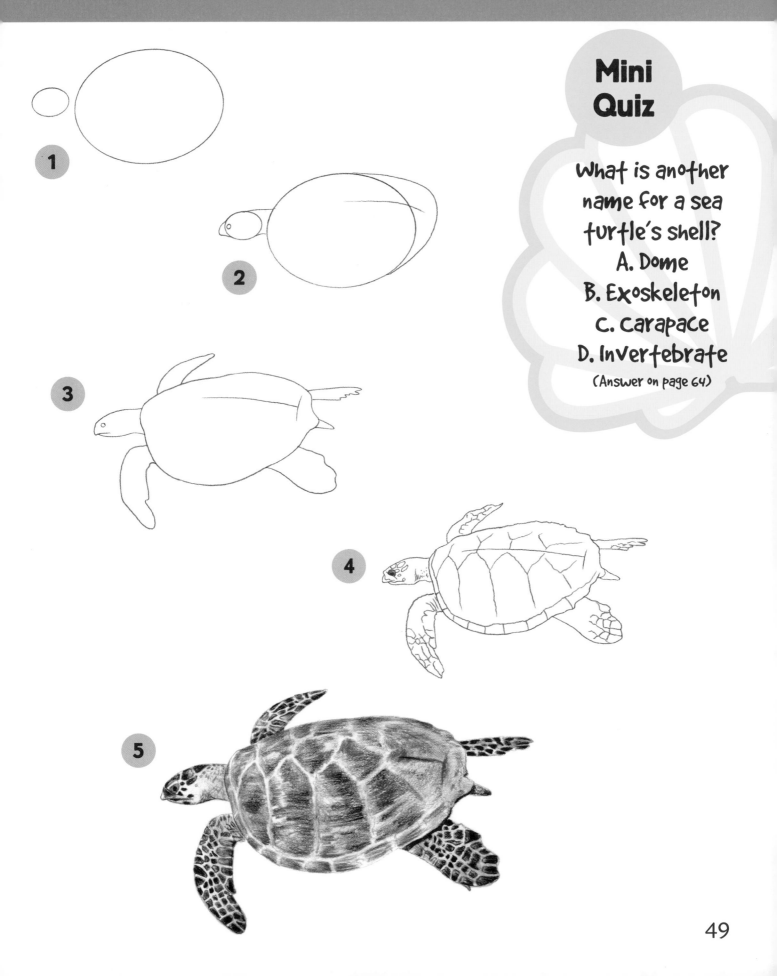

Mini Quiz

What is another name for a sea turtle's shell?
A. Dome
B. Exoskeleton
C. Carapace
D. Invertebrate
(Answer on page 64)

49

Spineless Cuttlefish

Details

Size: Up to 35 inches in length
Location: Tropical and temperate coastal oceans
Diet: Small crabs and fish

Cuttlefish are very similar to squids, with eight arms and flat bodies. They use two tiny fins along the sides of their bodies to skitter across the ocean floor.

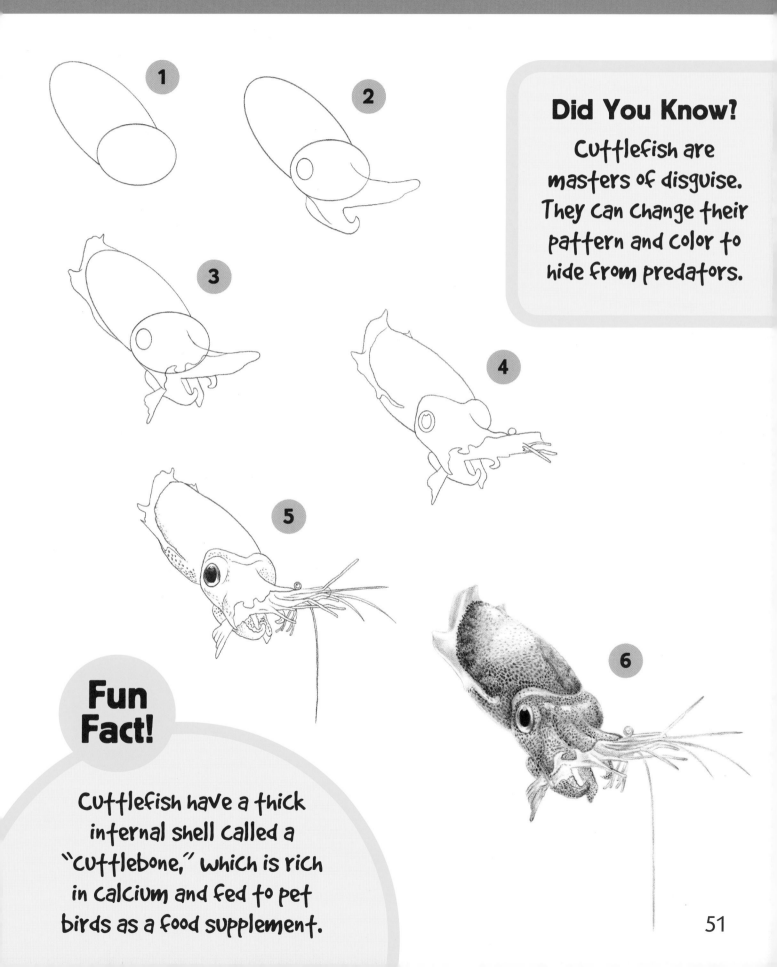

Did You Know?

Cuttlefish are masters of disguise. They can change their pattern and color to hide from predators.

Fun Fact!

Cuttlefish have a thick internal shell called a "cuttlebone," which is rich in calcium and fed to pet birds as a food supplement.

Squid

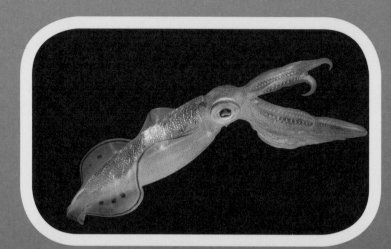

Size: From 1.5 centimeters to more than 33 feet in length!

Fun Fact!

The largest giant squid ever found was 59 feet long and weighed almost 2,000 pounds!

Location: Coastal and ocean waters

Diet: Fish, shrimp, and other squids

Squids are spineless cephalopods that have long bodies and short heads with big eyes that help them see in the dark depths of the ocean.

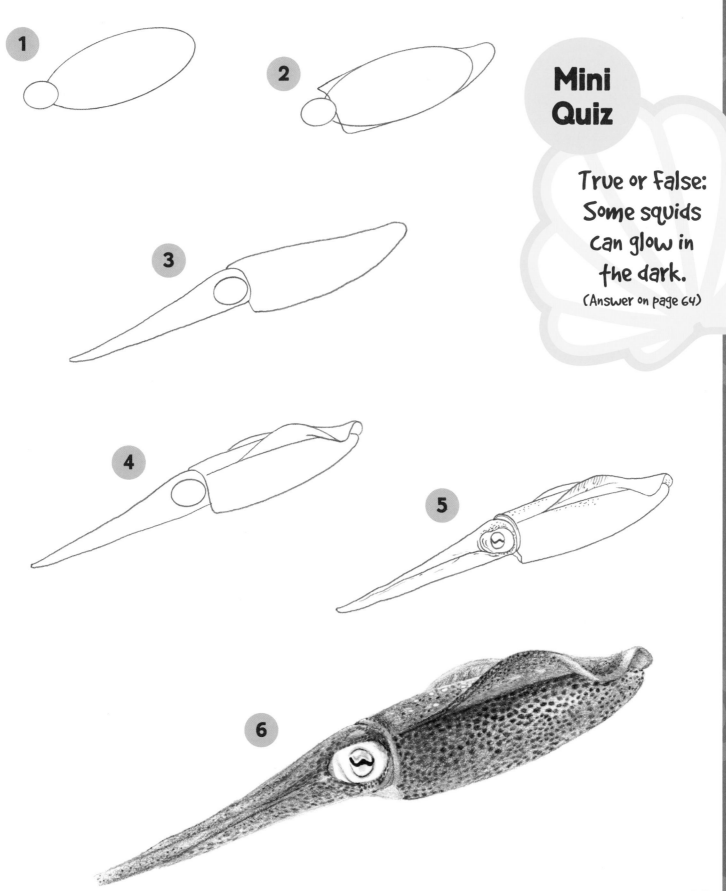

Mini Quiz

True or false: Some squids can glow in the dark.

(Answer on page 64)

1

2

3

4

5

6

Starfish

Fun Fact!

Sea stars, or starfish, are actually not fish at all. They are more closely related to other spineless sea creatures, such as sea urchins and sea cucumbers.

Starfish come in a variety of bright colors, and their skin is bony and hard, protecting them from predators.

Did You Know?

If a starfish loses one of its arms, it can grow a new one. The lost arm of some species can even grow into an entirely new sea star!

Stingray

Size: Up to 6.5 feet in length

Weight: Up to 750 pounds

Location: Tropical and temperate oceans

Diet: Shellfish, such as shrimp, mollusks, and clams

Did You Know?

A stingray's barb produces venom that is poisonous and can be deadly to humans.

Stingrays are very calm and docile, and they only use their sharp, barbed tails in self-defense.

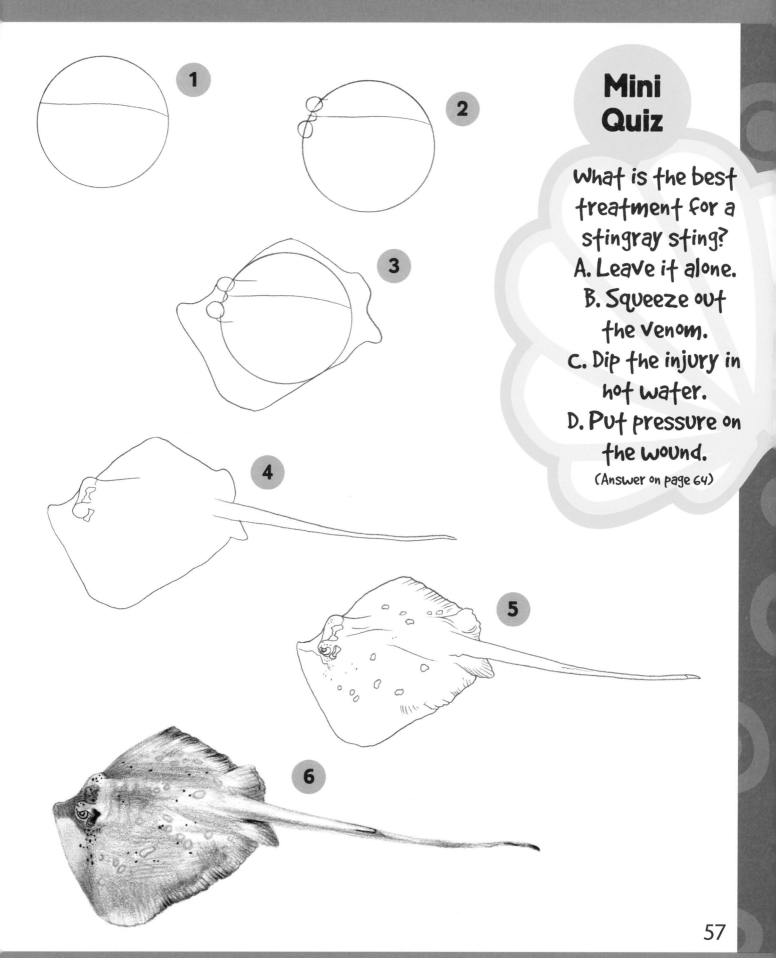

1

2

3

4

5

6

Mini Quiz

What is the best treatment for a stingray sting?
A. Leave it alone.
B. Squeeze out the venom.
C. Dip the injury in hot water.
D. Put pressure on the wound.

(Answer on page 64)

57

Swordfish

Size: Up to 15 feet in length

Location: Warm and temperate parts of the Atlantic, Pacific, and Indian Oceans

Weight: Up to 1,000 pounds

Diet: Fish and squid

Fun Fact!

Swordfish are incredibly fast swimmers—some can reach underwater speeds of 60 miles per hour!

The swordfish is known for its long, sword-like bill, which it uses to help catch its prey. Its smooth skin is blue on top and silvery underneath.

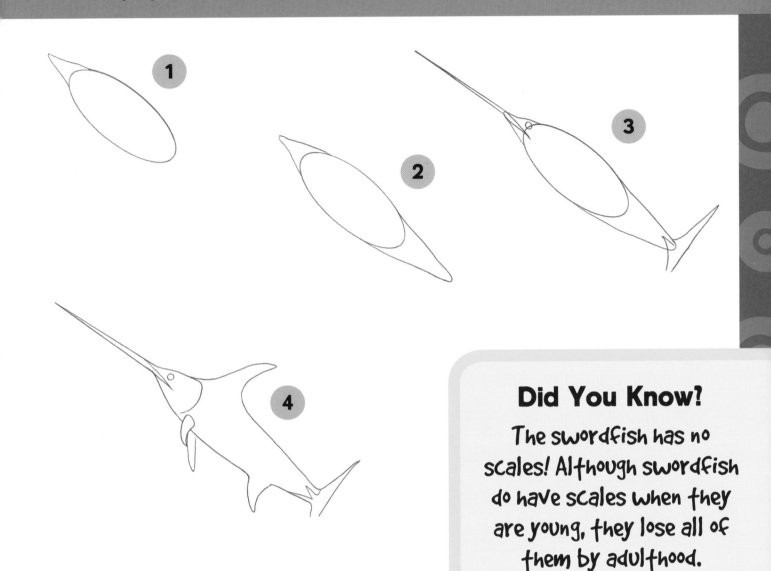

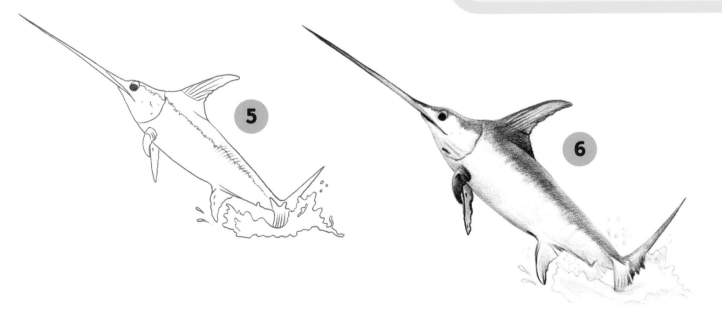

Did You Know?

The swordfish has no scales! Although swordfish do have scales when they are young, they lose all of them by adulthood.

Tiger Shark

Did You Know?

Tiger sharks are named for the vertical stripes they have when they are young.

Tiger sharks are known to be insatiable scavengers. They have sharp teeth and strong jaws that can crack even the strong shells of sea turtles.

1

2

3

4

5

6

Mini Quiz

True or False: The tiger shark's nickname is "Wastebasket of the Sea."

(Answer on page 64)

Walrus

Location:
Arctic Circle

Weight:
Up to 1.5
tons (3,000
pounds)

Size: About 10
feet in length

Diet: Shellfish,
clams, and
mussels

Fun Fact!

A walrus's long
tusks grow
throughout its
life and can be as
long as 3 feet.

Walruses have huge bodies full of blubber to keep them warm in the cold waters of the Arctic.

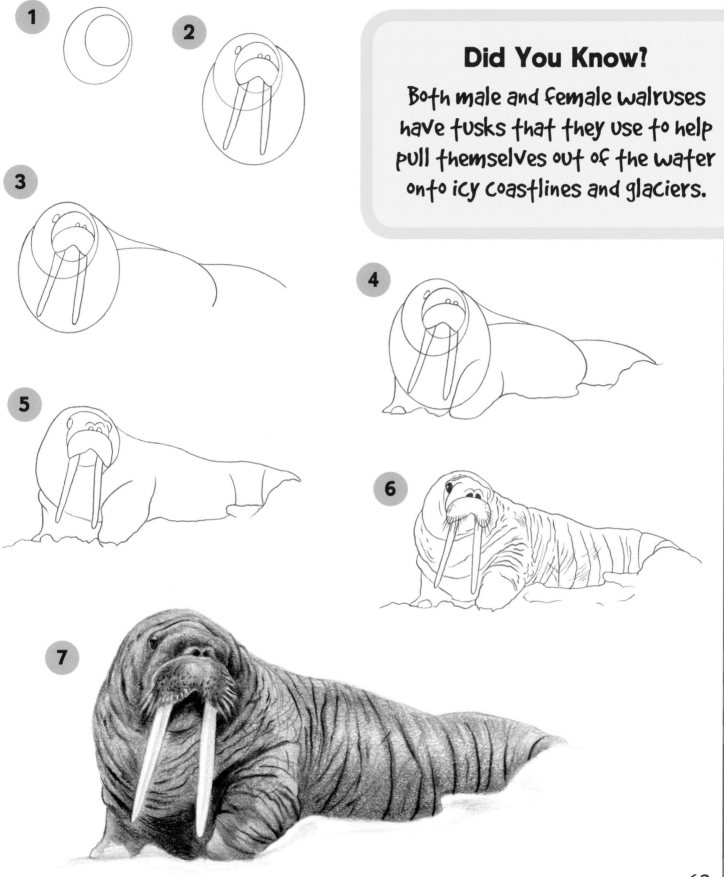

Did You Know?

Both male and female walruses have tusks that they use to help pull themselves out of the water onto icy coastlines and glaciers.

Mini Quiz Answers

Page 13: B. Dolphins are social creatures and often travel in family groups called "pods."

Page 15: True. Clownfish can become female if necessary, but once they change, they can't change back!

Page 17: True. Some species of crab, such as the horseshoe crab, have existed for more than 300 million years!

Page 19: D. The great white shark has an amazing sense of smell. It can detect blood in the water up to three miles away!

Page 21: E. There are a total of nine identified species of hammerhead shark.

Page 23: True. The lion's mane jellyfish is the largest jellyfish in the world.

Page 27: C. Manatees may be large, but they can swim pretty fast if necessary!

Page 33: A. Family groups of orca whales communicate through echolocation.

Page 39: True. Royal blue tangs use these spines for protection against predators.

Page 49: C. A sea turtle's shell is also called a "carapace." Although a sea turtle cannot pull its head inside its shell, the shell's hard surface helps conceal and protect the turtle's body from predators.

Page 53: True. Some squids have light organs that help attract prey deep in the ocean.

Page 57: C. Hot water helps neutralize stingray venom.

Page 61: True. Tiger sharks are known for swallowing anything they find.